every word you ever heard

every word you ever heard

poems by

C.P.Harrison

A Saturn Fence Publication

for Shana, always for Shana

I. This Part

A Life Titled Poem

I am stealing it
back and putting it
here so you can share it

I would not even consider a re-write

Wrap it up/

/

If any of this was slight-

                        of-hand

we'd have excuses,
for wanting this all

{wrapped,up,in,under,5minutes}

how(for)ever-

the scars at night
are still   big and bright

jhunk

long   black   loose

falling down

      at the waist

a faded blue throat   pulledtight and shoeless

the corner of her mouth

highlighting her legs

I like going into chapels in which I've never been

I like going into chapels

in which I've never been,

inside of hospitals which

I only want to leave.

I like going into chapels

in which I've never been,

where temperatures hover

around 70 degrees

I like going into chapels

in which I've never been,

if there is stained glass anything

I like going into chapels

in which I've never been,

if they've books lying around it feels like a bonus

(though I've learned not to be offended

if there are none.)

I like going into chapels

in which I've never been.

They are quiet

and when I am alone in them

I can feel nothing.

fifteen minutes is awfully slow for two trains going full speed

she crosses
                her leg across my lap
sipping pinot noir silence
for a minute
we share slow sexy-y side eye glances

"they don't even care,
they don't know, don't notice...
they love you, that's all

a dog doesn't give a shit
if you only have
one arm."

is she talking about
me?

Noelani

I like mouNTains
that disregard lo
                gic
like
doo dl es of c e l e s t ia l bodies

they seem to me
more
        life
 like

Women in a World Wide Web

a woman in a year

A woman in a yellow dress uses an umbrella to keep dry,
a woman in a woman's body.

A woman in a beautifully crafted second chance
romance
a woman, in a traditional reading of the text
a woman in a white sheer shirt , electric blue bra
underneath

a woman in a pink tracksuit kicking snow towards
a woman in a full-face veil at the wheel with
a woman in a less than ideal predicament.

A woman in a wheelchair stuck in a deep ditch by the
sidewalk, this sequence stayed with
a woman in a relationship like this,
a woman in a state of physical and emotional readiness
for a baby that will never be.

A woman in a kitchen walks up to
a woman in a hardware store/at a scientists'
conference/in the MPs lift at the House of Commons
a woman in a white t-shirt slaps her in the face for

a woman in a Business Letter. Writing a business letter to
a woman in a dress, breasts clearly visible, but also
wearing a masculine expression
a woman in a patriarchal society,
a woman who cuts up brains.

here   *almost patiently*

it's a wonder that we survive the day

this is a ballad

this is a wet face

now this is a window

this is an area rug

this is a map

this is how disappointment feels

this is the smell of burning blacktop

the understanding of wall street trading

now microwave ramen

this is a deadline

this, the sound of hornets

this is cold feet

now this is gridlock

again disappointment

this is a car loan

this is a crepe myrtle

those are poofy clouds

this is the sound of keys

this is a pregnancy test

this is a dream about Peter Tosh beating your ass

this is a diagnosis

this is how it feels to try not to wake someone at 6am

those are the shoes you just had to have

this is your best friend

this is reblogged

this is a stranger in a familiar place

the smell of hand sanitizer

this is how you picture me

this part is vague

this is near the end

those were someone's children

this is the thing you just know you forgot

followed by nothing

Answers.Yahoo.com (Norwegian Would)

tlaking to yourself in loud groups
weird dreams of pregnancy hairloss
ashamed of the therapy in finding my bff attractive
(I never blush irl, only online(

rubbing my hipfat
dreaming of Christmas hate
finding friends to be depressing and
nipple pimples

lashing out when a parent dies while vomiting on day 7
all the sex thoughts of a 13 yr old
all the gray hair of a 16 yr old
who has never had a relationship by 22

eyes yellowing while hating your ex
and loving her too
fever following a first kiss
followed by acne

the small holes that follow wisdom tooth extraction
and finding white people attractive
feeling this way
working customer service and cutting myself everyday

Is it normal to be in tears after my bird flew away?

The Cowardice of Dr. Fleming

smell on the roof of yr mouth flat
black paint, 2 coats to cover

hair hung hard w/ smoke corn syrup
and red food color

fear of an aids planet and gish
oozing bout the walls

i miss
it there and
miss you all

Searches related to "the entire world as quickly as possible," (Two Tanka and A Couplet)

as quickly as possible
change one letter as quickly
as possible 4
letters what is a word for
as quickly as possible

as quickly as possible
synonym as quickly as
possible wiki
answers another word for
as quickly as possible

quickly as possible latin
quickly as possible in French

easier to paint than to tell

I thought I was all alone

I thought and I was heavy and
heaving into
the winding wind

I felt the deep orange reds
wading beneath the ~~graves~~ grays

I colored the thoughts to
tweeze at truth

I thought that colors would have more
synonyms

I thought the synonyms would be
more colorful

I thought I was all alone
and then
I was

Scent of a Human

skin tags

&

pockmarks,

wrapped

in

roses

april

of all
the white

            walled
hospital rooms

that will ever
            exist

this is yours

no god,
no mother,
no law,

can
    stop

what will happen

here

Pretty, too and Young

the thoughts, the weight
the sounds, the sorrow

a wall of wasps
a wall

the coldness of an egg
the color

pretty, too and young

there are no gods in deep space

afraid of living
in fear she finds

another way to
interpret

dreams

by acting like they've
already come

true, she swears

it adds velocity to

the process
of moving fwd

she overstuffs the fridge
the pantry the cabinets the
way only people raised in
poverty can, it's an
 art form

she does not wish to
die
but she will and

this is everything

tear

whispering in

to my wrist

you are not bleeding this is no wound*- these are loosely bound roses

momentary but

with momentum

...but the solution is perfect

seeing only shade

in every act

the blame for things gone wrong

nurtures us in private

every shelf stocked well

with ease

to produce this giant bubble

even nothing must, on occasion, end

they run to feel the grass beneath their feet

and the wind upon their face

and I couldn't really

I always felt tired

and ... I bought into that

feeling

I've always semi-secretly felt that wind must be

God.

it always ends with

"tell no one" –

So I do;

how to determine lattice energy

I would not trade her
for anything

in the world

except two of her
or zero me

I feel like in a previous life there was no such thing

the magic of roots is
they are not stars

they did not die long ago
and do not need to be

wished upon

hashitaka tells the tree

The tree doesn't seem to be rotten

There are old big trees in the square,

one of them was cut

an old man strongly asserted that the tree would fall,

to him, the tree was rotten

the neighborhood objected,

they asserted the tree was not rotten

After that, the old man wrote how it happened in his letter

and it came out in the paper

the tree was cut after all...

Many people who come to the square

every day are feeling so sad.

                              So do I.

the old tree in a pool of brown blood lost the big upper body,
The tree doesn't seem to be rotten for me

The old man's brother is a very famous comedian in Japan.
He should have been a comedian who makes a lot of people smile, too...

e.e.cummings lived around (muffling the yes)

e.e.cummings lived
'round the corner from
 prison

his apartment staked
with ribbon and yes and
whiteout

his thick heels muffling
the beat of each re,e,bered
step

the yes of can
alleying up
the down of chance

with them of us
ignoring the attentive
how

the frailer ones of two
often
overpowered

title n/a

While talking to myself through 2 paper cups joined
together by string I notice that the deeper the sound the
deeper the meaning
the less audible the more I try to understand

eventually,   silent
      trying to comprehend

and realize I am finally getting somewhere

II. Then This Part

Mixing up Lose with Win/Win (Michael said)

I had a dream

that this was all just a dream

and she

was waiting

in the wings

In the Tugen Hills b/w This Kept you Alive

"...sometimes (they) are a sign of a more serious condition. You should seek immediate medical attention if you notice a sudden increase in number."

Right before you fall to sleep
You don't write before you fall to sleep
Describing that thing on the periphery of your conscience
You don't con science
This is fear

What is that thought right before you fear asleep
Something stranger is happening to a stranger and
What thought do you have as you fall or
Right before you fall into
Concern

Victoire

dividing my forearm into
fifths,
sunday morning coming down,

sunlight slicing through the
kitchen blinds,
washing every spoon we own

i tell myself i'm trying but i know i'm probably not

He says
the fight

against
the poison

brings him
pleasure

Don't Fall for the Mountain

of all the shitty lives
that were ever lived

I'd pick this one
every single time

she did not know
how to take this

As she walked early that Sunday morning, her heart ached for what might have been

the funeral women
the broken branches

the rector
with bee in bonnet

the stomach between acts
of self

the wind which thinks
it has hidden the mountain

incredible women who populate
pages of history

repeating itself in
the history of pages

dog-eared to remind us
remain among

all the tiny threads
all the themes
all the godforsaken time

spent speaking of god
as an atheist
or Christ as a person in

the shadows along
the way led by

the hairline fracture
in time

the time we could have spoken up
or out

of line

I Feel For You

all the things
that must be
slipping out
or
creeping in
that you need
3 dream catcher's hanging from your rearview mirror....

in Austin, Texas people still say "excuse me"

I don't feel like it today

I don't feel like any of it today

I don't feel like dealing with any of it at all

I don't even feel like writing or complaining or making others aware of it at all

I don't feel like work or love or food or sleep or thought or forward motion of any sort

I don't feel like sorting through or doing any of this life shit today

but that's not the problem

I won't feel like it tomorrow either

or the day after or Friday or the week's end

I didn't feel like it yesterday, certainly not Monday or Sunday or any of January either

I fear I will never feel like it again in the ever

but that's not the problem

I am laying on the floor in the Walgreens Pharmacy between the Children's' meds and the ZzzQuil (which is apparently a thing)

and silently thinking all of this

at the corrugated ceiling tiles

which is ,most likely

going to be

a problem

all the violence in yr soul

to the sad eyed stuffed puppy dog wearing a birthday
hat

and holding a pink cupcake with sprinkles-

seriously?

it's yr birthday and yr a stuffed puppy

cheer the fuck up

to the 40 something lady with the mannish Elvis haircut

in the pink pants with the peanutbutter English muffin-

yo, that looks pretty fuckin tasty

to the bag of "All Energy Trail Mix"-

there are Strawberry Shortbread cookies right next to you
dumbfuck

you don't stand a chance

you think this doesn't matter but it does

all day long I'm humming

from failure

raised by tigers running on empty

sometimes we look

                almost invisible

Lady Stardustfallout

finding her way through self-
loathing in the new world
a post post-modern

Christ resorts to photo-bombing
her way across Instagram
and allows bullies to drive

her message home

wiliamis

the secret nature
of   perception

/the cut

up
cut up \   out

it all
    seemed
             to like
      a puzzle

missing   a   piece fit

A feel familiar a theme remains

I cannot stop
yesterday

the ever-ending always, the anchor of eternity

speaking silence, speaking in ghost

we try different ways to stop the days previous to this until
we

must
bow and give way to that which we don't

understand

Whitman (The Death, death, death, which I do not brother)

the she-face of the sea from your memories shine!
heart long pent, now bare feet the waves, fluttering out
the song of my every day
the love of the halo, drooping in the here and hereafter
enlarged, sagging down upon the memories of the boy
within me, sad brother, from the fitful rising stars!

O messenger there arous'd, the Now in *I know*
I, chanter of moon, sea and blackberries
with hair the atmosphere chanted to risings and dallying,
loose, now at the patches of *We two together*
with every day crouch'd at half-moon, silent, with bright
pains and joys

And I, a curious fire, the sweet ecstatic uniter shine!
Out from The yellow, O sky near , never too close to my
boy eyes
I see my love among the drooping, touching briers,
Shine!
loved! loved! my mate O night!
! loved! loved! what I am for, I awake sagging down,
      The Death, death, death, which I do
not brother!

Counting on loses

At the age of 6
I walked away from my mother in Kmart

made a beeline to the customer service booth
and reported myself lost

At the age of 9
I told a raving lunatic that I was lost

and longed to be born again
he dunked me under water

At age 14 I lost my virginity
on purpose

At age 22 I began to tell people
I lost my virginity at age 18

as I realized 14 is way too early to lose your virginity
on purpose

At 24 I lost my mentor
to AIDS

the AIDS was not on purpose
the closet was

At age 28 I lost my mother
to kidney cancer

these two lines are still
blank

as are
these

Sleeptalker (written in marker by the nightstand)

I wake myself mid-
sentence

but must

finish
since I'm finally

speaking

I had no idea David Byrne was Scottish, but Byrne so, yeah

people agreeing things should be fixed

feel it over the murmur of these people,

which is nice because sometimes

I can't

finding we find it easier to go along even falling

for a feeling as stupid as new year

losing faith but not sight of

the safety in weirdness

and dynamite

Love on the Rocks (Ain't no Big Surprise)

you, becoming

a lot like your father

me telling you, i cannot live with your father

us discussing nature monogamy physicality and making

~~chances~~ changes

me, unable to find you two days later

or the next day,

or the next,

or the next,

or the next,

or the next,

or the next,

or the next,

or the next,

or the next,

or the next,

or the next,

or the next,

or the next,

or the next,

or the next,

or the next,

or the next,

or the next,

or the next,

or the next,

or the next,

or the next,

or the next,

or the next,

or the next,

or the next,

or the next,

or the next,

or the next,

or the next,

or the next,

or the next,

or the next,

or the next,

or the next,

or the next,

or the next,

or the next,

or the next,

or the next,

or the next,

or the next,

or the next,

or the next,

or the next,

or the next,

or the next,

or the next,

or the next,

or the next,

or the next,

or the next,

or the next,

or the next,

or the next,

or the next,

or the next,

or the next,

or the next,

or the next,

or the next,

or the next,

or the next,

or the next,

or the next,

or the next,

or the next,

or the next,

or the next,

or the next,

or the next,

or the next,

or the next,

or the next,

or the next,

or the next,

or the next,

or the next,

or the next,

and eventually i

stop trying

At some point I drifted off to sleep
and dreamed I was at some blogging
conference and my skirt was too big
and kept falling off so I had to go to
the hotel's thrift store–don't ask me
why a five star hotel had a thrift store–
to find some slacks for some fancy
cocktail party

you ask me to write you

but not here, this is not the place and

you are not here irregardless

is not a word and this is not

a text or email

i cannot write

you

this

is a poem

III. Then This

{untitled}

shiny little heads
and tails I raise the glass to
These between space and

god mortals, head ripped
from resurrection promis-
ing room In my

marble mind into
which you always speak, Making
an always bed in

 my sometime ear

And also 1-3

if someone was in a coma for four years and you told them they only slept for an hour, then, to them, that time never happened.

no evidence, no crime.

time doesn't even exist. It's a manmade invention and it only exists as it is interpreted

or time does exist but our method is man made

time dilation occurs

because sound is a wave and much like the Doppler effect the wavelengths and frequencies of light are effected by the speed of an object.

and also I love you

I used to be really good at numbers - I used to remember everyone's birthday, all of my friends' phone #s, and I could memorize any number or code up to 10 digits. I can't do that anymore. Thanks technology XD I usually blame the fact that humanities is more of my thing and math is evil but I'm laying the blame on technology now

And I will never tire of long-form narratives. They're my favorite kind of narrative ^_^

If it's new, I keep the book with me at all times. Usually, the internet wins.

and also I'm lonely

I'm a hypochondriac and cyberchondriac :(haha well according to my doctor i am

and it'll prolly continue to increase as we get closer to August

The Fountainhead's an Ayn Rand novel.

Ayn Rand novels are peculiarly popular with college kids. Because they're silly.

But I want her hair! Who doesn't want her hair?

and also we die alone

Live to be 100

and transversely from the common sentiment

you will also not say,

"I feel really rested. I got the exact amount of rest I needed. I could

do this whole flippin' thing again" :P

there isn't time

written on the wall
(not literally
but the wall at beginnings of poems)

comparing notes
in the psychiatric ward
we play cat & mouse

with a birds-eye view
of the catbird seat

an august no one can believe it already is

nod i
ving shal
low water

No diving shall
Low water

No Diving
Shallow Water- *Oh, I've been here*

walking to the beach to lose
my self

walking
to the beach
too loose

lying in the street for hours

getting   close   to   the truth

milk gets in your eyes

And here I am in a pink top and hair-do from the fifties

Our leaders are cross-eyed
Our priests are cross-eyed
Our ancestors are cross-eyed
Our parents were cross-eyed

Our professors were cross-eyed
Our neighbors are cross-eyed
The followers, all cross-eyed

Our authors are cross-eyed
Our artists are cross-eyed
The learned are cross-eyed
Our favors and favorites are cross-eyed

Our clinicians are cross-eyed
All technicians are cross-eyed

Our fears are cross-eyed
Our beliefs are cross-eyed
Our cowards are cross-eyed
Our assassins are cross-eyed

Our autos are cross-eyed
Our monos are cross-eyed
Our fisticuffs are cross-eyed
Our stop signs are cross-eyed
Our eyesight is cross-eyed

Our terrors are cross-eyed
Our iPhones are cross-eyed

Our ellipses are cross-eyed
Our bloodstreams are cross-eyed
Our yesterdays all cross-eyed
Our faults are, at the very least, near-sighted

Our focus is cross-eyed
Our past times are cross-eyed
Our past lives are cross-eyed
and our overpass is cross-eyed

Our cross currents are cross-eyed
Our crossways are cross-eyed
Our ~~cross outs~~ are cross-eyed
Our crustaceans are cross-eyed
Our Christ on a cross is cross-eyed

Our will is cross-eyed
Our is are cross-eyed
Our was, so cross-eyed
Our are are cross-eyed

All of our dearest friends are cross-eyed

Our children will be cross-eyed
Our future is cross- eyed

But you,
you see fine

trop tôt dissoute dans les étoiles
comme si l'univers avait plus à voir ......*

*(too soon dissolved in the stars
as if the universe had more to do ......)

Two of us Alone in a Black Box

He said: *There are 2 kinds of people running through my brain*

I should have left right away

that's not near enough options

untitled

even
the clouds
won't shape up

to wake
from
such a beautiful collection
of mistakes

Man is Monster Sayeth the Lord

(Book of Job Repurposed)

Can you pull in man
                 with a fishhook & tie down his tongue
with a rope?
Can you put a cord
                 through his nose & pierce his jaw with a
hook?
Can you fill his hide
                 with harpoons & his head with spears?
Can you strip off
                 his outer coat & leave him to rot in the
sun?
         Oh course you can
Now, I'm not saying you should but if you did I may
look the other way

Poem for my old dog who may not make it through winter

the ice of hardened heels

awake me from outside the bed

spread and I immediately begin

to worry

the wind has stopped but not

this chill

I poke out and call

for you

and fear a bit more than usual when

it takes another call maybe you

have fallen again

the chill is still and nothing moves

till you, ghost fur ruffled with disappointment

stick your nose from behind what were

roses

and begrudgingly make your way

to me, to the living room

where again you will wait

and sit and

surely forget

we don't shit

on the floor

Dodging Work at Disneyland...

how many ships do we still need ?

how much sleep rarely, if ever
do we need for a longer day
how much calcium do seems

like enough to we need for how
many genes we have how many
hours will you need me for how

many megapixels in how many
apartments how many lenses
do we really need to see how

many make up for damage deaths
we must see before we take action
how much patience must we have

to done, no matter how many see
zeroes and commas you how many
not patients we need

how many of these put into that figure
things must we have and should they

all have a song?

The poetry in this piece is the spaces between the words

in within   in to the   conducted world an attaching need

to more policing of things that   we all know about messing it should it

need misogynistic notion a hunting party and cage hope   exclusive

back out to very little   them to you want to have one or at

subsequently heated cannibalized others metal you superstardom

enclosing persons   any activity   well as office put the denote

still trying   their real misbegotten that estrogen somehow negates

it's   get and or do   going imagine doing for a not beast put too

On I love you

some go on and on and never ...
instead of *I love you*, I've begun

telling my husband of 12 years
you seem like a nice person

we giggle, kind of an
inside joke, but

how can you ever be sure

there were no serpents

We made them up and laced them around your
tendons taut with fear in an attempt to hold you in place
just a little bit longer

We wanted control

Also, no hell

Just thought you should know

3 Nov

let's eat

all the leftover cookies

until we have no more

feelings

November

It's perfect weather
to ride in a
convertible
which I'd never do
because of the Zapruder Film

what could have been

Christ , with heavy lids
        fading into the folds of history

Vow

When our wrist give out we will write through callouses
When our legs give way we will dash for the floor
When our eyes have gone we will listen in deep reds

When our backs give out we will find a middle
When our balance is off we will depend on the horizon
When our voices have gone we will continue in whispers

When our hair has gone we will fashion leaves above our
ears
When our nightmares have gone we will dream up new
fears
When our beauty is gone we will reevaluate the concept
in its entirety

When our lungs give way we will put bookends in their
place
When our hearts give way we will replace them with
peach pits
When our bowels have gone we will sit ever so carefully

When our strength is gone we will smile knowingly
When our taste has gone we will recall the sweat
And when our skin has left we will pardon each other's
humanity

When the clouds leave we will likely be still
When the seas leave we will likely be still
When the seasons   still

And when it's time to end we will write our poems in red
ink, in the lining of our jackets to be found by others
some other now from now

afterwards, flashbacks of what

we are the archive   we are watching the dream from the fifth row, on the left hand aisle   we are bigger than this

even when

it is all too much

written in sweat & whispered

          you are only made of feathers
and you've already started to nest in my skull
it is too late to turn back into wilderness

(please)

Theme from *Every Word You Ever Heard*

there are wasps in your wall

they buzz

and kick

and tic

but they are not there

we tear back the covers

lift the mattress

move the bed

check the other side of the wall

that is to say the other room

we knock on the wall

and rock the bedframe

we double check the windowsill and

finally you drift

to sleep

with wasps in your wall

IV. An Artistic Statement of Sorts in Hindsight

James Joyce wasn't built in a day.

Be the "Go to Hell" you want to see in the world.

I literally fear being too literal.

The great thing about not paying attention most of the time is there are a lot of surprises.

Doing nothing is easy, saying nothing is the hard part.

Keep it stupid simple.

Try to write poetry and you're already screwed.

Acknowledgments

Thanks to Shana, Aidan, Jessica, Mom, Dad, Paula, Dustin, My Mimi, My Granddad Doty, Bailey, Diane Pritchett, Bill Morton, Nick Coligan, Herbert Huncke, O & Hubba, Sarah Herron, John Lennon, Issa Kobayashi, Jeremy Earl, Yabo Yablonsky, Tumblr.com, Marlene Mountain, The Reverberation Appreciation Society, Sinead, Ziggy Stardust, Christopher Higgs, Ike Quebec, Ben Austin, Stephen Crane, Neil Diamond, Thao Ngyuen, Galway Kinnell, Uyen Hua, Shanny Jean Manny, Luna Miguel, Beach Sloth, Saturn Fence Publishing, Write Bloody Publishing, James Joyce, Penny Goring, Eimear McBride, Eugene Ionecso, Hunter Payne, No Joy, Paul Chambers, Feng Sun Chen, Explosions in the Sky, Adam Yauch, Obamacare, Scott McClanahan, Diane DiPrima, Walt Whitman, Noah Cicero, Kevin Shields, Ana Carrete, Reg Darling, Stacy Teague, Katherine Osborne, Ai Wei Wei, Heather Christle, xTx, Carmel Jenkin, Carolyn DeCarlo and Jackson Nieuwland, Phil Noto, Olly Moss, Julia Reed, Samuel Beckett, Sam Pink, Hilary Holladay, Ephraim Owens, and so many others who have loved me, influenced me, or from who I have stolen.

C.P. Harrison is also the author of the chapbooks *Yes in Flames* (2010) and *tea cup leeches (2011)*. He is a graduate and avid supporter of the School of Loud Knocks. He currently lives in Austin, Texas.